The names in each group are always in Latin or Greek because
these two languages are un... ... ...
the world.
The examples shown on th... ... ...
the Southern Elephant Seal ... ... in.

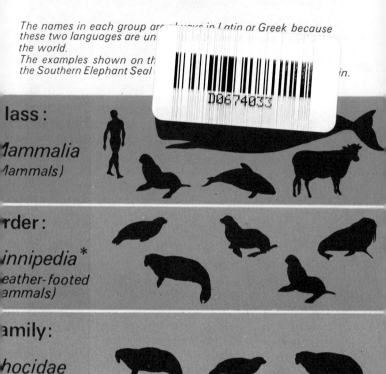

lass:

Mammalia
(Mammals)

rder:

Pinnipedia *
(feather-footed
mammals)

amily:

Phocidae
(True Seals)

enus:

Mirounga
(Elephant Seals)

pecies:

**Mirounga
leonina**
(Southern
Elephant Seal)

*The order Pinnipedia was
once regarded as a
sub-order of Carnivora
(flesh-eating mammals), but
is now accepted as a
principal order.

to teachers and parents

This is a LADYBIRD LEADER book, one of a series specially produced to meet the very real need for carefully planned *first information books* that instantly attract enquiring minds and stimulate reluctant readers.

The subject matter and vocabulary have been selected with expert assistance, and the brief and simple text is printed in large, clear type.

Children's questions are anticipated and facts presented in a logical sequence. Where possible, the books show what happened in the past and what is relevant today.

Special artwork has been commissioned to set a standard rarely seen in books for this reading age and at this price.

Full colour illustrations are on all 48 pages to give maximum impact and provide the extra enrichment that is the aim of all Ladybird Leaders.

A Ladybird Leader

seals
and whales
and other sea mammals

written and illustrated by John Leigh-Pemberton

Ladybird Books Ltd Loughborough 1976

Harp Seal, *Arctic Ocean,*
1.9 m (6 ft 3 ins) long.

The animals in this book
live all or part of their lives
in water.

They are all *mammals.*

This means that
they feed their babies on milk,
are warm-blooded and breathe air.

Walrus, *Arctic Ocean*,
3 m (10 ft) long.

Millions of years ago
they were land animals.
They gradually took to life
in the water.
Limbs changed into flippers.
Lungs, ears and eyes
        have changed too.

Pilot Whale, *N. Atlantic and Pacific*,
7.6 m (25 ft) long.

Seals

Seals are flesh-eating animals.

They live mostly in the cold seas
of the world.

They eat fish, shellfish
and other sea animals.

Except for the Baikal Seal,
all seals drink sea-water.

Seals are covered
with a layer of fat.

This is called *blubber*.

Blubber protects the seal
from the cold.

Some seals have
a double coat of fur.

They are known as *fur seals*
or *sea bears*.

Fur Seals, *Pacific, Indian
and South Atlantic oceans,*
are sometimes more than 3 m (10 ft)
long and weigh 1000 kg (2205 lb).

Sea Lions

Fur seals have been much hunted
for their thick fur.

Far too many have been killed,
so now some kinds are rare.

Sea lions have only thin fur,
so they have not been
hunted so much.

Steller's Sea Lions. The male is
much larger than the female.

Sea lions are found mostly
in the Pacific Ocean.
The large Steller's Sea Lions
give a long, bellowing roar.
The cry of the young
is like the bleating of a lamb.

Eared seals

Fur seals and sea lions
are known as *eared* seals.

This is because their ears
can be seen.

Other seals do not show
their ears.

Instead, they have just
a small slit in the skin.

Californian Sea Lion diving.
This is the seal most often seen
in zoos and circuses.
Even in the wild
they are playful.

Eared seals have longer necks
than other seals.

They can move their hind flippers
backwards and forwards.

The other seals cannot do this.

Eared seals : how they swim

Eared seals spend
much of their lives at sea.

Some travel long distances.

They use their front flippers
for swimming.

They can swim at about
20 kph (12½ mph).

They can dive to depths of
more than 100 m (328 ft).

Eared seals: how they live

Huge herds of eared seals
gather on rocky shores
or small islands.

They always come ashore to breed.

These breeding places are
called *rookeries*.

The pups do not swim
for at least a fortnight.

True seals

Seals which do not show their ears
are called *true* seals.

They cannot move
their hind flippers forwards.

So they do not move so easily
on land as the eared seals do.

Common Seal, up to 2 m (6½ ft) long.
Both these seals are found on
all North Atlantic coasts.
Their pups are white at birth.

Grey Seal. The male *(bull)* can be
3 m (10 ft) long and weigh
290 kg (640 lb). The females
(cows) are smaller.

Seals in Britain

Two kinds of true seals
are found in Britain.

The Grey Seal lives mostly
on rocky shores.

The Common Seal likes
sand banks.

Ribbon Seal, up to 1.7 m
(5 ft 8 ins) long.
It is rather rare.

Arctic seals

Some kinds of seals live
on the ice of Polar regions.

Five kinds live in the Arctic.

They are hunted by Eskimos
and by Polar bears
and killer whales.

Bearded Seal,
up to 3.7 m (12 ft 2 ins).
It has a very loud voice.

Ringed Seal –
The smallest seal,
up to 1.4 m
(4 ft 7 ins) long.

Harp Seal –
The best swimmer of all seals.

The young of these true seals
are born on the ice.

Their mothers feed them
on very rich milk.

They soon become very fat.

Hooded Seal,
up to 3.5 m (11 ft 6 ins) long.
The 'bag' on its nose is
inflated when it is angry.

Antarctic seals

Seals which live on the ice
make holes in it.

They do this in order to be able
to breathe and to catch their food
in the water below.

The hole has to be kept open.

The seals do this
with their noses and teeth.

Weddell Seal using an ice hole. This, the
largest Antarctic Seal, can grow to 3 m (10 ft) long.

The Leopard Seal, up to 3 m (10 ft) long.
It is the fiercest of all seals.
It feeds on penguins and
other seals.

Some seals spend the winter
below the ice.

They stay in ice caves.

They breathe through cracks
in the ice.

The Crab-eater Seal, up to 2.5 m (8 ft 3 ins) long.
It eats shrimps - not crabs. It has special teeth
which act like a sieve.
It can move across snow at 24 kph (15 mph).

How true seals swim

True seals swim
by moving their hind flippers
from side to side.

They use their front flippers
for 'treading water'.

Monk Seal,
up to 3 m (10 ft) long.

Monk Seals

The only true seals
which live in warm seas
are the Monk Seals.

They live in Hawaii
and the Mediterranean.

Freshwater seals

There are seals in Lake Baikal in Siberia.

It is 2414 km (1500 miles) from the sea.

It is filled with fresh water which is frozen all winter.

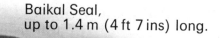

Baikal Seal,
up to 1.4 m (4 ft 7 ins) long.

Seals' eyesight

All seals have marvellous eyesight.

This is because they find much of their food in deep water where it is dark.

Elephant Seals

These are the largest of all seals.

One kind lives
in the North Pacific
and another
in the South Atlantic.

For three months,
during the breeding season,
the males do not feed at all.

Bull Elephant Seal,
up to 6.5 m (21 ft 4 ins) long,
and up to 3500 kg (7716 lb) in weight.
The nose can be blown up
like a balloon.

Elephant seals can dive
to great depths.

They can stay under water
for about twenty minutes.

On land, they can stop breathing
for five minutes.

Walruses

These large animals live
in the North Pacific and Atlantic.
They feed on shellfish.
They dig these from the sea bed
with their tusks.

Walrus. It can be 3.5 m (11 ft 6 ins) long and weigh more than a tonne.
Walruses can dive to 75 m (82 yds).

Walruses live in large groups,
often on rocky islands.

Their loud bellow sounds
like the bark of a big dog.

Eskimos hunt them for food,
leather and the ivory tusks.

Sea Cows or Sirenians

Manatee,
up to 4 m
(13 ft 1 in) long.
It lives in
the Caribbean
and in West Africa.

Sea Cows are
another kind of mammal.

They live in the sea.

They eat only water plants.

They can stay under water
for fifteen minutes.

In former times, sailors thought
that they were mermaids.

Dugong, about 3 m
(10 ft) long.
It is found round
the Indian Ocea
and in Australia

Sea Otter,
about 1 m
(3 ft 4 ins) long.
They eat shellfish
and crabs. The pup
is carried on its
mother's chest.

Sea Otters

Sea Otters do not have
a thick layer of blubber
as other sea mammals do.

So, to keep warm,
they have a double coat
of beautiful thick fur.

For this they were once hunted
until they had almost become extinct.
(*Extinct* means that
there are none left.)

Whales

A whale's tail is horizontal,
not vertical like a fish tail.

Whales are mammals
which live all the time
in the sea.

They are quite helpless
if stranded on shore.

Whales are of two kinds.

There are *toothed* whales
and *baleen* whales.

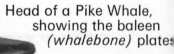

Head of a Pike Whale,
showing the baleen
(whalebone) plates

Pacific Striped Dolphin, up to 3 m (10 ft) long. This is a *toothed* whale. Dolphins are just small kinds of whale.

Baleen *(whalebone)* whales have no teeth.

Instead, they have rows of *plates* hanging from the roof of the mouth.

These plates act like a sieve.

They trap tiny shrimps called *krill* on which they feed.

Krill.
There are many kinds.
Millions of them
swarm in the sea
where the
baleen whales
feed.

Blue Whale

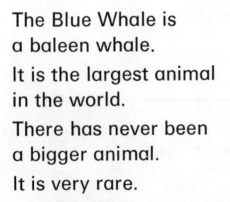

The Blue Whale is
a baleen whale.

It is the largest animal
in the world.

There has never been
a bigger animal.

It is very rare.

Found all over the world.
Can be 30.5 m (100 ft) long,
and weigh more than 100 tonnes.
There are fewer than 2000
Blue Whales left.

For many centuries
man has hunted whales.

He has hunted them for oil,
meat and whalebone.

Far too many have been killed.

So now all the great whales
are becoming fewer and fewer.

North Atlantic Right Whale,
about 15 m (50 ft) long.
Right whales are
almost extinct, due to
over-hunting.

Right Whales

Right Whales have huge heads.

Their plates of whalebone
can be 4 m (13 ft) long.

They are called *Right* Whales
because when killed they float.

So they were the *right* sort
of whales for hunters to kill.

How Baleen Whales feed

Baleen whales feed by swimming with their mouths open.

They take in a lot of water in which the krill (page 29) are floating.

Their tongues push out the water.

The krill are trapped
in the baleen plates.

Finback Whale, up to 24 m (80 ft) long.
It can swim at 48 kph (30 mph).
It travels from
one end of the
world to the other.

Breaching

Although they are so huge,
whales are very active.
This great Hump-backed Whale
weighs as much as
thirty tonnes.

Even so, like most other whales,
it can jump
clean out of the water.
This is called *breaching.*

Blowing

The nostrils or *blow-holes*
of whales are on top of
their heads.

When they dive, whales close
their blow-holes.

Baleen whales have
a double blow-hole.

Toothed whales have
a single one.

Grey Whale, about 12 m (40 ft) long.
Once almost extinct, it is now found,
and protected, off the Californian coast.

When a whale comes to the surface
it blows out the air
from its lungs.

This warm, wet air looks like
a jet of steam.

This is called *blowing*
or *spouting.*

Toothed Whales

Toothed whales do not have
plates of baleen.

They have teeth instead.

They use these
for gripping their prey.

They eat octopus, squid
and fish as big as sharks.

The Sperm Whale or Cachalot

The biggest toothed whale
is the Sperm Whale.

It has about fifty teeth,
all in its lower jaw.

Sperm whales can dive
to 900 m (nearly 3000 ft).

This deep dive is called *sounding.*

Sperm Whale, up to
20 m (66 ft) long.
Found in warm oceans.
It can stay under water
for an hour.

Killer Whales

These are the fiercest
of all ocean animals.

They are the only whales
which prey on birds, seals,
and other whales.

They can break ice
one metre thick.

Killers (or *Grampus*) make
huge jumps out of the water.

They can leap 13 m (43 ft).

They hunt in packs.

Packs of whales are known as
schools of whales.

Killer Whale, found in all seas.
Males are up to 9 m (30 ft) long.
Females are much smaller.

Beluga or White Whale,
with young,
about 4 m (13 ft) long.
It lives in the Arctic.

Whale voices

Whales have rather poor eyesight
and no sense of smell.

They have very good hearing
and sense of touch.

They make many different kinds
of sounds.

These sounds help whales
to keep in touch with each other.

They make whistling, moaning,
squeaking and warbling sounds.

The Beluga makes sounds
very like a bird's song.

It is often called the 'Sea Canary'.

Narwhals

Narwhals live in the Arctic.

They have only two teeth.

The left-hand tooth grows out
through the upper lip.

It forms a twisted tusk
up to 2.5 m (8 ft 3 ins) long.

Narwhals grow to 5 m (16 ft 6 ins) long.
The female's teeth sometimes
never develop at all.

How do whales swim?

A whale swims by moving its tail
up and down.

Whales' tails are known
as *flukes*.

The flippers are used
for steering and balancing.

Beaked Whale.
Found in most
oceans, it is
about 8 m (26 ft)
long.

Why are whales so big ?

Whales live a long time
and grow to a great size.

This is partly because they live
floating in the water.

They do not have to support
their own weight.

Bottle-nosed Whale.
A big whale, 9 m (30 ft) long,
it dives fastest of all
whales and can stay for
hours at great depths.

Blubber

Because they live in cold water, whales have to be protected against the cold.

They have no fur.

So their bodies are covered with a layer of oily fat.

This is called *blubber.*

In some big whales the blubber can be 35 cm (1 ft 2 ins) thick.

Baby whales

Whales produce quite large
single babies, called *calves*.

The calf is born under water.

It must be able to breathe,
so the mother at once pushes it
to the surface.

Whales feed their calves
on milk.

At first they are sometimes fed
on the surface.

Later, they suckle under water.

They stay with their mothers
for more than a year.

Dolphins and porpoises

Common Dolphin,
about 2 m
(6 ft 6 ins) long.
Found round
Britain and
world wide.

Dolphins and porpoises are
small, toothed whales.

There are many different kinds,
found all over the world.

Some dolphins live in rivers
in China, India and South America.

Pacific Porpoise,
about 1.8 m (6 ft) long.
Like most dolphins
and porpoises, it
lives in *schools.*

White-beaked Dolphin,
about 3 m (10 ft) long.
Common in
British waters.

La Plata
Dolphin,
1.5 m (5 ft).
It comes from
S. America and
has more than
200 teeth.

Dolphins are very intelligent,
inquisitive and playful.

They will swim alongside a ship,
leaping in and out of the water.

Dolphins have *beaks,*
but porpoises do not.

Common Porpoise,
about 1.8 m (6 ft) long.
Found throughout
the North Atlantic.
It does not leap from
water as much as dolphins do.

Index